Hermosa

Yesika Salgado

Salgado, Yesika

1st edition

ISBN: 978-1-945649-33-2

Edited by Safia Elhillo
Proofread by Rhiannon McGavin
Cover design by Cassidy Trier
Editorial design by Ian DeLucca

Not a Cult
Los Angeles, CA

Printed in Canada

for Saya
and all the brown girls of Los Angeles

you are blooming, my love.

Contents

my love,

tonight I have my house to myself. the jacaran-
da tree outside my window is blooming. it is May in Los
Angeles and I am more beautiful than I have ever been.
my lips are painted hot pink; my nails are long and gold;
my favorite love songs are playing loud. I have a stack of
poems piled next to me: about love I have found and lost,
about my city, about my joy, my grief. I have gathered my
disasters and triumphs for months and held on to them as
long as I could but it is 1 a.m. time to give birth.

every story begins this way: the night stretching
before me and an impossible knot of words waiting for
my hands. I don't know what the other end will look like
but I know I will find myself there. I hope within these
pages you are also able to find your own beauty, what calls
you home, what sets you free. this, like everything I do, is
my heart calling you back into yours. I give you the final
chapter in this trilogy of what makes us beautiful and
whole.

in full bloom,
Yesika

mira loca, vení,
tell me about that time again

where you were free,
where you made a mess,
and were forgiven
the way we forgive the men

Diaspora Writes To Her New Home

I am what comes after the civil war
after the dismembered corpses
the burnt sugar cane fields
the mango tree strung with a single hanging body
the man with his tongue in his pocket
the soldiers and the guerilla
the exodus of my grandmother's children

I arrived after the fleeing. after the bruise was named a
desert. after the new country extended its concrete arms
with reproach. after living in garages. huddling in small
apartments. after raising blonde children who do not
know our language. after washing cars we do not drive.
after keeping home for women with alabaster skin. after
falling in love in the time of asylum. after the alcohol took
to my father's veins. after the family murmured his sins.
after my mother cut the long coil of her curls.

I found my way here and stayed. a fist of a girl with eyes
big as a wailing mouth. I was born with a pen under my
tongue. I know and own all words ever spoken. I am the
dream and the nightmare. the burning bush. Moses. David. Goliath. Mary Magdalene.
The Holy Virgin.
God himself,
dead and resurrected.

I am not the survival
I came after.

I am the victory
a boastful flag.

I am not a promise. I am a threat.
I am what takes and does not give back.

a new history
a forked tongue
a priestess
church and communion
a woman with her own legacy

take this, my story.
eat it and remember me.

Casamiento

let's get married when the jacarandas are in bloom. when
the lotus flowers on Echo Park Lake have stretched into
open hands. make me yours during summer. beneath the
Dodger Stadium fireworks. the night air my veil, the 101
tail lights sequining my gown. my bouquet a palm tree
borrowed from Sunset Blvd. let a procession of lowriders,
priuses and rapid buses lead us to our reception. a hun-
dred street vendors with their hot dog or elote carts lining
the street, feeding those that celebrate our love. let's have
our first dance to a Snoop Dogg song while the neon
lights from a liquor store shadow your beautiful face.
someone setting free a dozen ducks taken from MacAr-
thur Park. let's make Pershing Square our dance floor.
borrow the mariachis from their plaza. Exposition Park
the centerpiece to every table. promise yourself to me
on Slauson on Cesar Chavez on Temple on Vermont on
Parkman. I have seen enough of the world to know that it
has always been you. I return to you with open arms. my
beautiful city. Los Angeles. I choose you in this life, in my
parents' lives and in the lives they left to bring me to you.

Sacrilegious

this is a church I built
there is no God here

I burned the bibles and hymns
all statues lie on their backs
I am dressed in lace kept for altars

in this temple,
there is no woman weeping at a man's feet
the apostles were sent off, asked not to return

the wine remains. it is still blood.
I offer it with manicured hands

religion keeps folks warm at night
and my lovers know
the creed of my bedroom,
sweet sacrament of thighs and mouth

there is only choir, one song:
moans
venerating my
blessed flesh

Your Lipstick

you're always wearing it. on purpose. you like the way
it colors your face. your mother only wore hers for very
special occasions. the same tube of soft pink every time.
you—well, you are not like that. you have all the colors of
a sunset in your makeup bag. the boys ask you questions:
is that for me? can I kiss you? can those lips be mine? and
you remember when your mouth was just a mouth. not
a target or a weapon or some kind of home for lost men.
you continue wearing your red. deep red. hot pink. violet.
burgundy. blood red. blood orange. blood. *where is the
party?* someone asks when you board the bus. you don't
smile. you are the special occasion. you deserve more than
one tube of soft pink smeared timid across your lips. you
re-apply your blood. you are a bruja now. you are the one
that makes everyone in the novela cry. you look out the
bus window. you wear victory so well.

Ever After

we did not work out. that's fine.
the years will take care of the ache.
what we learned of each other is still alive—
go be happy;
come tell me about it someday

La Cita

third date / we sit at my favorite bar / I listen to him talk
about another woman / it's fine / I'm only here 'cause I'm
trying to forget someone too / and isn't that dating in Los
Angeles? / fighting through traffic / only to arrive at places
that remind you of someone who broke your heart / hop-
ing someone new likes you enough / to break your heart
again / my date laughs / it's a loud laugh / fills up every
corner of the room / the one I'm trying to forget laughs
loud too / see? / everything is a comparison / later I tell my
girls maybe we want to be single / the new men don't stick
because we won't let them / they agree / we go out danc-
ing and all come home / together / this isn't forgetting /
this is writing the story / without any traffic

I Think It's Okay

if I never forget you. if you're forever a puncture in my
lungs. if I go around wheezing your name. like a dusty ac-
cordion. I think it's okay. I can survive like this. someone
will ask about my greatest love. I'll squeeze out a song. I'll
tell them I don't know what became of you but I remem-
ber your hands on my skin. and that is enough. together
we learned that love isn't peace. I let you go. I can live like
this.

The Jacaranda Tree

I just want my own place / somewhere to burn sage / I
want to play music loud / have it sweep the floors for me
/ want mangos and avocados on my table / walls the color
of ripe fruit / couches soft as a lover's belly / I want to
keep the door open / a small garden outside / a jacaranda
tree just beyond the fence / I want to hear the highway
in the distance / mistake its roar for the ocean / I want
the ocean nearby / mistake its whistle for a highway /
I want windows with no blinds / yawning into a night
sky / tear-streaked on rainy afternoons / I want books
on every surface / a kitchen that smells like coffee / pots
and plates that clink together / oven full of skillets and
pans / my niece and nephew's drawings on the fridge / I
want a bear that was born a dog asleep beneath my desk
/ I want to call him something silly / like baby or tiny / I
want picture frames on all the shelves / a phone ringing
every afternoon with my mother's voice / candles I light
when I am joyful or melancholy / most of all I want to
find a home that isn't you / isn't us / isn't that quiet room
where we died / where I left all hope of you coming back /
announcing that you choose me after all / instead / I want
my own place / doesn't that sound so / nice?

Invocation

a woman loves a man and life begins.

the man does not love the woman
and she writes a world in which he does.

that is the spell.

you might have happened.
I might have dreamt you up.

but there is a book about the way
your kiss made my mouth water
and I held your hand on the same street
where I learned to ride a bike

we stood beneath the lemon trees
where my father used to pick fruit
our goodbye was in the alley
where the first boy
I ever loved
cupped my breasts in both hands
brought them to his mouth
sucked them like mango seeds
and gave them back

that is the spell.

I asked for love to come and go.
it's been happening all along.

A Different Ending

let's say it worked. you became boyfriend that became
husband. I had the babies and named them after planets.
we built a house out of straw. you kept your bottles. I kept
everything else. we tied our relationship out in the yard
with our parents. two angry dogs that barked day and
night.

you still hold me like I can break.
I still cry during sex.

but it's love. you and I.
we are a mess. you and I.

let's say it worked. we got the life I planned for us. you
work all day. I don't write anymore. I don't travel. I raise
the kids. I keep my anger. you keep your drinking. the
dogs bark so loud I can't hear you. the dogs bark so loud
we stop kissing. the dogs bark so loud you start looking
like my father. I leave like your mother.

let's say it worked

we kept each other

along the way,
ruined
everything else.

Marathon

touched the scar / asked how it found him / he says
gunshot / I say nothing / we make love / he walks to the
bathroom / small crater on his side / it tells me to go
back home / to my gentrification / fenced gardens / quiet
streets

long time ago / bullets often sent me home / police
flashed lights / into houses / cars / eyes of boys I loved
/ I got lucky / we lost the block / *it got safe* / *it got better* /
everyone moved away / in pickups / or handcuffs / they
left

my lover is no longer my lover / he finds his way to my
street / drunk and determined / *come outside* / I don't know
what I fear more / what happens when I step outside /
what happens if I stay inside / it isn't safe for us to be
human here / we argue beneath a street lamp / I feel the
whiteness panting against the windows

Nipsey is killed / I text my ex boyfriend / *I love you* / *please
be safe*

and my block is quiet / so fucking quiet

Appendage

take the mangos
the lemons
the trees I can't climb
take the jacarandas
their purple promise
take it all

leave my legs
these swollen stumps
I do not hate yet
although they've slowed me down

one last letter
from my father's diabetes

perhaps a warning

who knows

they swell like the ocean does at night
my toes ache, my bed calls,
I do not go
I write my poetry
with their salt

Reservoir

I think of Mami crossing / the border / the purple sky above her / the desert / deep blue blanket stretched out at her feet / she tells me she saw La Virgencita out there / I imagine Mami walking through Mexico / everything dark and slow / like underwater / had to hide her Salvadoran accent / already leaving that country behind / I don't know much of Papi's crossing / I know the civil war made him run / the other day my cousin said *this country broke your father* / I know / Papi was going to be a doctor before El Salvador began to eat itself / his first home here was a garage / he showered with a garden hose / Papi was a quiet man / until the alcohol loosened him / that fire water washed him into something new / I am a happy drunk / I dance / talk / feel free / in ways I don't any other time / it scares me / how good it tastes / I was born in Los Angeles / raised in Silverlake / back when all the families were brown / all I ever had to cross was my English / the Spanglish one into the good one / I could sound white over a phone / Papi and Mami always said my papers gave me an obligation / I had to go to college and get a career / I didn't go to college / I do have my career now / I still live with Mami / Papi did another crossing ten years ago / I imagine that world blue and purple and slow too / an endless sea stretching between us / when Papi visits my dreams / I am always by an ocean / I don't know if it's Santa Monica or La Puntilla / he visits me and we are underwater / I tell him I crossed into a new place / I smile / it's a new smile / it is sure of itself / he doesn't recognize it / he touches my face / I wake up in tears / Mami is in the kitchen / I hear the water running / waiting for us

Boomerang

when you come checking on me,
know I haven't fallen into the fire.
I pick myself up, say *I can still do it without him.*

when I heard you had a new girlfriend,

I didn't imagine her body. didn't wish my own away.

instead I worked. planned. opened a savings account.
wrote. smoked on cold nights. drank on good nights.
cut off twelve inches of my hair. took pictures. booked
a cruise. flew to San Francisco. lay in a bed with white
sheets. called men I stopped calling when I loved you.
bought jewelry. took myself to dinner. the movies alone. a
bar alone. went to concerts with friends. stood close to the
stage. sang loud with my face to the sky. my skin as soft as
you left it.

when you come checking on me,
when your palms itch at the sound of my name,
know that I haven't fallen into the fire
instead, I became it

Hidden Track

she can have you

a new song
I keep on repeat

Dilluvio

4 a.m. you want me to come outside and hug you.

it is 2019 and the world is underwater. it is not supposed
to rain in Los Angeles. but the valley has been flooding all
week. the palm trees lining Sunset Blvd are waterlogged.
my legs and eyelids are swollen. I beg you to let me sleep.

4 a.m. is too late and too early to do anything.
but here you are. and I don't want you to be.
you say this is love. I say this is a torrent.

I can't tell stories about men without mentioning my
father. *my greatest love. my largest scar.* he had caramel eyes
like yours. and when you lean in like this. alcohol swelling
in your breath. you smell the same.

4 a.m. becomes 5 a.m. my arms are crossed and your
hands are in my hair. a year ago this would have been the
poem.

there are small storms and there are hurricanes. we have
been both. *I am here.* you say. as if this is the ship we both
have been praying for. there is nowhere to go. your lips
taste like salt. the neighbors turn their lights on. my voice
cracks. I am no longer made of unrequited love. it rained
for days. you are what the sky washed up. it is too late.

I Taught Him To Say Yes

years
I whispered
each letter
into his
sleeping ears
rubbed them into his palms
kissed them over
his cherrywood skin

and when he

finally

said yes,

it was to someone else

Red Line

I am wearing my favorite shirt / it is cropped / made of turquoise lace / I smell good / expensive / I am ruining my makeup with tears / my acrylic nails digging into my palms / I am not lost / the next stop is home / what does that matter? / there is a woman standing with a body thinner than mine / I think you would like her / I think to her you would have said yes / a stranger is smiling at me / I wonder what train the woman that loves him is on / what shirt she won't wear again / what truth she learned today that she'd rather turn in for a lie

Coven

I call my best friend after my fight with him
ask her if I was overreacting
I mean, I'm right to feel the way I do, right?
I'm not crazy like he says I am, right?
he calls me that all the time
crazy,
says I'm tripping
says I make something out of nothing
says he's here, isn't he? doesn't that mean anything?
I'm crying and she's listening
she's so good at listening
she's the first person I called
when Papi died
when the boyfriend before this one cheated
when the first baby died inside me
she listens until I finish sobbing
then, tells me what I swear are magic spells
I stop apologizing for loving what doesn't love me
I can feel my feet again at the sound of her voice
I can wiggle my toes, I can walk away
we change the subject, *hey guess who I saw?*
who? I ask
the gossip finds us
we talk until our throats go raw
like two hearts wrapped up in chords
call me tomorrow, ok?

Relapse

it is too cold
to be alone
I am drunk
and spent all night
being touched by men
I wish were you
I think of your bed
the stain on your carpet
your neighbor next door
who coughs all night
I call you and
I touch myself
while we talk
your voice
a hand curled around my throat
I love you
I miss you
I am sorry
please come back
I moan
finish before you do
lie in the dark
pretending
I haven't
isn't this the story of us?
we hang up after you are done
again, the story of us

Blood Right

I used to sell knives door to door
worked a parking garage booth
was a salesperson in a paper goods store
developed 30-minute film
called folks about refinancing their homes
nannied a pair of twins
became head cashier at another drugstore

I'd take the bus to each job
all of them out west
in Santa Monica
or Palisades
or Westwood

I used to commute
three to four hours every day

I know this city
the way I know heartache
I can taste it
before I can give it words

I mourned my father on the 704
I got my test results about infertility on the 302
I wrote the first poem in my first book on the 201
broke up with plenty of boyfriends
over the phone at bus stops

made my way to the beach
contemplated walking out into the water
but I always came back on the last bus
counted the purple trees on my block
kissed my mother's cheek goodnight

gentrification tried to tell me
that what once loved me
can no longer love me back

and I laughed

you can't take what's in my blood.

Barren

I gave my first book to the world
and miscarried a child the same month

the third time motherhood
pulled its hand from me

the long-faced doctor
sat me down
said
difficult - unlikely - high risk

I let my hands curl around each other
for once, I did not cry

I rode home with a stranger
did not tell him
that children do not want me

my lover asked
if I'd ever give him kids
I opened and closed my mouth
blinked

why would I do that?

Alone In Los Angeles

missouri was a blur of pale faces
north carolina, a humid kiss
georgia left mosquito bites on my thighs
washington looked like a bare hand
kentucky and nevada were slow and quiet
oakland was a melody
I recognize but
could never hum on key
modesto could have been mine, but wasn't
like san jose
santa barbara,
san diego,
your bed
the summer sky
a single palm tree framed by the window

all places
I have been
without you

including
here
in your bedroom
next to you
deep
within
myself

Tontita

vení aquí mi niña tonta
mi lloronsita
mi corazónsito roto

¿porque lo quieres?
¿porque lo buscas?
¿que te dio que te tiene tan perdida?

claro que lo amas
¿como no lo vas a amar?
si él fue el primero que te dijo
que quería todo lo que tu has querido

yo sé que es bonito
consentir a quien uno ama,
tener a quien cuidar

pero mi niña loca
mi palomita triste
mi cielito gris

ese hombre no quería ser querido
el lo que buscaba era olvidar
y tu mi amor, tu no eres el olvido

¿te acuerdas de tu Papi?
de ese amor tan grande
de las tardes bajo los palos de limones
y tú y él hablando de las noticias
o de algún deporte
o de un compañero de trabajo
y de vez en cuando
tu chiquita linda,
le preguntabas
¿Papi como se dice tal cosa en español?
y él te contestaba casi riendo
y tu seguías con tu cuento

¿te acuerdas de ese amor?
¿cómo puedes amar a alguien que no te puede dar lo mismo?

corazón,
dime
que te trae
tan mariada
por un hombre
que jamás te amo
como te enseñaron a amar

dime, que yo no lo entiendo

Punchline

I ate his ass because I loved him
gave myself lockjaw sucking dick,
swallowed the bitter cum
nodded when asked whatever he asked

I let him eat my pussy all wrong
I moaned in the name of romance
arched my back
pulled him in for a kiss,
his heart was in the right place.

later I laughed with my friends
I don't exactly know
what the joke was,

his awful sex

or me
neglecting my body
calling it love

Dos Con Todo

what is love?

it is 2 a.m. the lights in the club have come on. you are
tipsy, sweaty. your lover presses his hand into the small of
your back. guides you out into the street, past the crowd
and straight to a hot dog vendor. he leans over you and
says: deme dos con todo por favor.

what is falling out of love?

it is 2 a.m. the lights in the club have come on. you are
tipsy, sweaty. your lover walks ahead of you into the street,
past the crowd and straight to the car. you ride home in
silence. he drops you off. you get into bed. alone. drunk.
hungry.

Mi Malestar

when the world
is finally asleep

there you are

terror of my nights
my wicked hunger
insomnia in my bones
my precious curse
the sting in my jaw
bitter and sweet
colic of my heart
its bloody thirst
its wet mouth
saying
your
name
like a rosary
long after
someone's
died

The Fever

do you love me?
how much?
for how long?
what if someone better comes along?
what if I gain more weight?
what if I cry too much?
what if I call too often?
do you still love me?
I asked you yesterday, but what about today?
have I scared you off?
do you think of me?
do you want me?
do you mean it?
do you love me?
what parts?
show me, where?
do you love me?
where? show me.
I can't hear you over myself.
what is it? tell me.
do you love me?
yes?
I don't understand.
tell me, again, why?

My Lover Asks

because I love him
I consider straightening
my hair when he asks

because I love him
I shaved my pussy
before going over

because I love him
and he hates makeup
I don't wear any when I see him

I tell a friend that he thinks I'm beautiful

we both believe my lie

What I Remember Of Love

laughing with my mouth pressed to his bare shoulder /
pulling over on Beverly to point out the full moon / my
hand curled around his / a six-hour fevered confessional
on xmas eve / smiling so much my face hurt / ironing his
work shirt / his voice at 3 a.m. / never speaking over me /
listening even when he disagreed / drunken phone calls
to murmur he loves me / reading the same book / having
different opinions about its ending / Sade playing while
we make love / calling each other when work feels point-
less / crying into his lap / making bets about politics / ar-
guing but never leaving / knowing he sees me / all of me /
and still stays / back then / when I knew him / before / he
knew someone else / when distance became an aftertaste
in each kiss / when I forgot what his snoring sounds like /
when it got so complicated we stopped trying

I remember love. it's all I ever do.

Culver City

we slow danced,
once

it was mid afternoon
in your apartment above the trees

you pulled me
out of a poem
I was memorizing
and into you

a song I had
never heard
was playing

your chest
smelled of cedar
and I made a home
for my lips
within its bark

years later
when my friends
say they hate you
I laugh

I don't tell them
that some nights
I try and picture
what the trees saw of us
swaying in the sunlight

did it really look like love?

Luna De Miel

where? where do you love me?

here
in the skin behind ears
in the pits of both arms
in the parts
no one finds beautiful
but I do

I love you
here
and here
and
here

Madrugada

he wakes up halfway through the movie
reaches through the blankets for my hand
his eyes soft and heavy from sleep
hello beautiful
and
I glow
in the dark
brighter than
the screen

Dick-Sucking

the first time
I took you into my mouth
we both
lay in your bed
a strange geometry of limbs
the sheets were blue
and the moon
colored the walls

I imagined we were underwater
and the only way
to stay alive
was to finish
what we had begun

I went home that night
throat swollen
and the smell of you
in my hair

my driver
must have known
I had just earned
my legs
and entered
this world

Florecer

you kiss my neck
and
all my pores
sprout
flowers
every hair
I own
is now
a dandelion
I am
no longer
myself
but instead
a garden
and you
the hands
that turn
my soil

Daggers

first date
looks at my long nails

ten sharp knives
I wear like jewelry

ever clawed up a man's back with those?

we excuse ourselves
to take them
for a drive

It Never Snows In Southern California

I wish Los Angeles had winters
the Hollywood sign covered with snow
ice on the roads, frozen water in the pipes
the ocean turned mush,
air too cold to fill anyone's lungs
reasons to say,
don't leave
the world is ending
and I have a bed

Hexed

in high school
Mrs. Brooke looked at me, said

be careful. girls look for their father
in the men that they love.

I laughed

and never shook her curse.

Costumbres

sometimes, after Mami, my sisters, and I were gone for the day, we'd come home to a drunk and angry Papi. would know before we even got in the house. a pot full of spaghetti sprawled across the front steps. the door smeared with tomato sauce. all the lights on. couch cushions thrown around the living room. the phone yanked out of the wall. Papi asleep in a chair. snoring. we'd quietly clean the mess. coax him to lie down. turn off the lights. tip toe into bed.

you call. tonight. I can hear the alcohol before I hear your voice. *are you up?* my stomach sinks. sometimes you want to talk about us. all the words I never get to hear jumbled on your lips. I listen. drunk words are still words and I've been so thirsty. you can't tell I'm crying. if you do, you don't acknowledge it. I let you tell me how I do everything wrong, why I don't deserve your trust, why we are the way we are. I coax the sweetness out of you. ask what I don't dare ask the sober you. let you talk yourself to sleep. I quietly gather myself. turn off the lights. tip toe to bed. fall asleep to the sound of your heavy breathing.

Ya Casi

your parents say goodbye while they're still sitting at the
dinner table. they stand with their keys in their hands and
say it again. they move to the door and say it some more.
then the driveway. when the car turns on. your tío leans
a hand on the window while they keep saying goodbye.
mami forgets something and runs back inside. they all
stand by the car some more. you fall asleep a little bit. you
wake up and they're still there. you get back out of the car
to play with your cousins. papi calls you back. tío smacks
the car one time, tía waves and you know you're leaving
for real. finally. you wish they had kept saying goodbye for
a bit longer.

when you grow up and are a full adult. in love. and love
goes sour. you threaten to leave. you sit at the table and
say *I am gone.* some days pass, you stand with your keys
in your hand. you swear you're going to do it. weeks later
you make it to the door. say goodbye some more. make
it to the driveway. your lover leans in. promises the right
things with one hand on your thigh. you linger but you
swear it's only for a little. grow numb and forget about
breaking up. it's like you fall asleep. settle into staying.
you're all in again.
but remember why you have to go.

this time it is real.
finally. you are gone.

you wish your goodbye had taken longer.

Dark Humor

say the word dead enough
and it becomes a joke

my father is dead

spill it onto the table
during a date
and watch their cheeks flush

my father is dead

unfold it like a chair
when asked
if your parents
are proud of your
new career

my father is dead
dead
dead
dead dead dead

and the room flinches
the lights dim
you laugh the kind of laugh
that tastes like sandpaper
but fills a silence

you continue telling whatever story you were telling
it's fine. we're all gonna die eventually.

ha. ha?

Milagros

one time,
when I worked in a parking lot
I couldn't wait to get home
so I walked up Montana Street
where I had keys to an empty office building

I let myself into the bathroom
lay on the tile
slid my hands down my pants

without thinking of anyone
I remember the orgasm
my uniform
hands under the cold water
washing the smell
off my fingers

that's when I used to belong to myself
or maybe when I was most lost

either way
the world was ending,
and I could make myself cum
like I was racing death
and always won.

The Almost Death

did I tell you
about the time
I was dying?
about my uterus
that couldn't stop bleeding
the doctors blaming my fatness
and me agreeing
did I tell you
about the times
I couldn't get dressed
because I was more crime scene
than anything
about this bloody curse
the stains on couches
showers
underwear
bus seats
that black paste of my sex
my vulva, a wound that wouldn't heal
I almost
lost all of myself
ounce by ounce, once
I ended up in an emergency room
the doctors couldn't understand
how I let it go that long
how I didn't think anything was wrong
they found a growth
hemorrhaging
I never saw it
but I imagined it looked
like an urn
the thing that held my fathers ashes
the last place I ever saw him
the doctors paraded in and out
reaching between my legs

dozens of men pulling my lips apart
shaking their heads
I've been here before, I thought
on my back on a bed
a man disappointed.
my mother called relatives
told them I was sick
referred to my vagina
as "down there"
the beast that can't be named
the sin that must be whispered
a red river down my legs
a soiled gown
a dirty secret
I stopped dying then. it took a while,
first came the blood transfusion
then the clamps clawing open my cervix
me, strapped to a bed
screaming in pain
thinking of women
who endure this
and it isn't to keep them alive
but instead to make them a little more dead
how lucky I was,
my body more forgiving
it started talking to me
asking,
why was I so afraid of her?
why didn't I trust us?
hadn't we buried my father a year before
and made it out intact?
hadn't we put down our fists and given up the bruises?
hadn't death asked us
over and over again
if we were sure we wanted to stay?
hadn't we said yes every time?

didn't it try to take us anyway?
didn't we stay alive?
aren't we alive?
my body said.
alive.
listen to me
are you
not
alive?
and I started renaming parts of myself
calling them what they needed to be called
my sex, my pussy,
my jewel
my sweet fruit
my loved orchid
my come here lover,
come celebrate that I am alive
that I once almost wasn't
come, taste
what staying
is like

The Trick

today I am not a writer. I am my halted Spanish and
insecurities. I am fingers that know letters but not gram-
mar. my only degree is my library card. I read someone
else's words and shrink. turn into a speck of envy. don't
know how not to weigh my work against theirs. can't stop
feeling like I am a cheap magician's trick. if I move too
quickly I'll give myself away. you'll learn, I am only stack-
ing these words together to pull myself out. I don't know
how you got here. I wasn't trying to save you. all I have
been doing is staying alive.

Metro

the safest seat is behind the bus driver
you can find your way anywhere by asking
if you get lost, take any bus that says Downtown LA
the sun sets west, home is the other way
the 4 runs all night
Rapids don't make every stop
if you're gonna cry, choose a window seat
headphones and a book will protect you
from unwanted conversations with men
if you're gonna cry, stare down at your phone screen
have someone you can call during late night rides
if you're gonna cry, do it quietly
if you're gonna cry, do it into a sweater
if you're gonna cry,
leave a trail of tears
between work and home
let them wash your tired feet
cry for the heartbreak,
the shitty job,
the dying parent,
the angry friend
the loneliness
give the city your sorrow

rain is always welcome in Los Angeles

Exile

there are parts of the city you haven't visited in a while
cause all you do is work and sleep and work. one day
you wake up feeling nostalgic and take the bus to Grand
Central Market and it doesn't look anything like you
remember. the taco stand that made their own tortillas
is missing. so is the man with the 5o¢ ice cream cones.
there is a white couple eating pupusas with forks and no
rancheras playing anywhere. a knot in your throat. you
don't know who to tell about this sadness. the only brown
face you see is the woman sweeping around the tables
and she's too busy to listen to your broken heart. the last
time you remember being here was after your father went
into a coma and you ate a slice of pizza and some Mexican
coconut candy to swallow the panic. the ladies with their
mandados sitting around you. you closed your eyes pre-
tending they were your tias and you were safe among your
people. but now it's all different. this was a part of the city
you never thought gentrification would want. you are los-
ing the places that made you. there are white people here
and you aren't. you're already somewhere else. but where?

Papi In Five Parts

the first one
is a quiet
Sunday afternoon

I find myself
holding his hand so often
there is no need
to tell him I love him

at dinner
I prefer to eat
from his plate
instead of mine
and he never stops me

he is tender
so tender
I pretend to fall asleep
with my head on his chest
just to hear his breathing

as if I were inside of him
a vital organ
as if this were the reason I was made

he calls me his heart
and I never doubt it

I know
the second one
has come home
by the slam
of the door
it is three a.m.
and every light
is on

his music
loud and angry
like him
when I ask
what's the matter
beg him to go to bed
he answers
in sounds
like a
hand slapped
to a face
or a body
slammed
to a wall
or glass
broken
to a cheek
I try
not to cry
because
my tears
are like blood
to a shark
and he is a shark
in the deepest
part of night
my name caught in his jaws
there is so much yelling
I wonder why the police
haven't been called
so much anger
I fear
the sun
won't rise
in time
to save us

the third one is full of jokes
that sound like insults
his humor as cheap and easy
as the vodka he likes

the fourth one
never remembers how much he's hurt me
when we bump into each other in the kitchen
the next morning
he won't look me in the eye
his apologies come as a
hurried kiss to a forehead
a mumbled I love you
before he rushes off to work

I resent him
sometimes even hate him

It is so difficult to love him
but if I don't
who else will?
who else will forgive him?
who else will save him?
who else will make him want to change?

the fifth one
I wished for
every single day of my life

In every blown out birthday candle
every time I knelt in a church pew
I begged God to send him to me soon

and when he did
when God finally gave me a sober father
he was so brittle
broken
apologetic
so willing to make it work

I had no choice
but to forget
everything that had come before him

the day he left me
a sudden exhale of wind
a slight twitch of a foot
a hand I wouldn't release

I remembered the first one,
the little girl
pretending to fall asleep
with my head on my father's chest

as if I were an appendage
of his body,
the reason I was made,
as if he had never become anyone else
other than the man who called me his heart
and never let me doubt it

Eden

the first time I smoked weed was in the name of love.
Ricardo was a cholito with eyelashes that curled on their
own. I was down to do anything for him. it was third peri-
od when we both leaned our heads over an apple turned
pipe. he talked me through the inhale. I looked up into
his eyes, almost forgetting to exhale. we hid in the base-
ball field until the bell rang. when we walked to class I did
not know if I was high or if I was floating. maybe both.
we got to algebra class, Ricardo leaned in and through
the fog I heard him say *hook me up with your homegirl.* I
was back on earth and in my fat girl body again. the apple
should have given it away.

The Seizure

Silky came running home
his leash dragging behind him
when Papi didn't show up
& Silky scratched at our legs
we knew something was wrong

out on the street we three
ran in different directions
yelling *Papi! Papi! Papi!*

one of the borrachitos
pointed under the bridge
there Papi was,
a small mound with a swollen tongue
I am not drunk. I am not drunk.
the words stained my hands

the other two ran to the liquor store
came back with a candy bar
we fed to him
there
on Silverlake & Sunset
with cars honking
& folks walking by
& Silky's leash dragging behind him

my sisters & I
stood our father up
one under each arm
another, the dog in her arms

let's go, before Mamí comes home

Big White Building

remember
the motel
where we used to jump the fence
just to blaze between school periods?
the one on Sunset and Bates
where I cried when I saw
that the boy that I loved had tagged his name
and next to it
a girl's name that wasn't mine?

they've turned it into a piece of art
it's white and bright
people take pictures in front of it all the time
I think it's because it reminds them of snow
and we don't get that around here.
remember the bus stop next to it?
where you asked boys to meet you
so you could walk into school holding hands
and I'd shuffle behind you
my face in a book
you'd laugh at my weirdness
the boys laughed too.
that building wasn't white then
I think it was tan and red
like me.
I think of those days
they wouldn't have painted
the motel white
back then,
these streets still had too much brown

Hermosa

Papi bought my sisters and I uniforms. lined us up on the front steps. tallest to shortest. *Miren a mis hermosuras.* took a polaroid and drove us to school. we were the only kids in white polos and blue shorts. I am sure this is a metaphor for many things. his drinking. Mami's legal status. their service jobs. the smart daughters they were raising. three beautiful medallions. polished. new. our good English in our backpacks heavy as bricks.

Judas

I was seven years old the first time / a poem / got me in trouble / it was about my father / punching my mother / it was true / sometimes the truth is also a lie / sometimes it doesn't set you free / it sets you up / your father / calling you Judas / the rest of your life / my father / taught me to love words / to read everything I could get my hands on / my father / taught me / words have feet / say the wrong one and it'll run as far as it can / announcing itself / a word / stops being yours / once you say it / I did not stop writing poems / I am running too / I go far ahead of myself / on sheets / on screens / I am now in places I have never been / this must be freedom

Bayunca

I had a tía that would sometimes drink a beer and play
poker at parties. the other mujeres would murmur. beer
is a man's drink. milk and coffee is for the mothers. they
drink their cafecito at a table while talking about fulana
de tal or aquella bayunca que se cree mucho. I'd sit as
closely as I could and listen to the gossip. memorizing
names of all the scandalous relatives. the tío with kids
from a secret woman. the cousin who left to Mexico cause
he got in trouble here. the loca that is off acting like a
man again. those were my favorite stories. women doing
what women don't do. I imagined all the beer I'd drink
when I got older. I'd chug it down like a cold soda and
burp loudly on purpose. I'd cackle big and booming.
wouldn't care when the mujeres say ¡esa niña es tremenda!
instead I'd lift another beer and say ¡asi es! ¡salud!

Memorization

I can walk down the block with my eyes closed
I can draw it for you on a napkin

the building that looks like a castle
then the two identical blue apartments
the white one where Cheli lives
Blanca's house and all its kids
turn at the front gate of the next one,
walk past the first door, we don't talk to whoever lives
there,
then Don Pablo's house
then Ana's with her loud abuelita
down five steps
past the basement with graffiti
past the mailbox
that doesn't hold
my terrible report card - thank God
between the lemon trees
say *hi Papi!*
Poppa's hands and newspaper sitting in the shade
Mami's face at the kitchen window, kiss her cheek
peek into the bedroom
Jenny reading Harry Potter on the top bunk bed
Julie watching TV from the bottom
the living room clean and quiet
a square of sun on the floor
Selena singing about dreams

Mami yells at me
for dragging jacarandas into the house

look at my shoes—
there,
crushed into the sole
is a garden
I brought home

A Beginning

I was born.

sometimes I want that to be all the story there is to tell.

I was born and there was a parade. or fiesta. Mami came
home in a gown and I was the corsage on her wrist. Papi
chugged down a beer, stuck two fingers in his mouth and
whistled. my tías laughed, tíos drank. the cousins old
enough to hold me passed me along. one pair of hands to
the next.

she is here! she is here! la niña is here!

if only that were it, but
I was born and the story had just begun

Tan Tan!

my eternal gratitude to Daniel Lisi. Ian DeLucca. Cassidy Trier. Safia Elhillo. Shihan Van Clief. Javon Johnson. Katrina Kirpatrick. Joel Jaimes. Gabby Rivera. Zoila Darton. Pablo Simental. the hands, eyes and push that brought me to the page. I would not have arrived to this trilogy and finished it without any of you.

Marshawn Lakes thank you for your grace while I insist on writing books that also carry your story. I love you, in full bloom.

Jennifer and Julissa no manuscript is done without your names being written in it. always, the power of three.

Adela Palacios y Jose Elmer Salgado. mis corazones. mis tesoros. mis hermosuras. este es el fruto de nuestro amor.

colorin colorado. mis mangitos, este cuento se ha terminado.

About the Author

Yesika Salgado is a Los Angeles based Salvadoran poet who writes about her family, her culture, her city, and her brown body. She has shared her work in venues and campuses throughout the country. Salgado is a four time member of Da Poetry Lounge Slam Team and a 2017 and 2018 National Poetry Slam finalist. Her work has been featured in the *Los Angeles Times*, *Latina Magazine*, *Univision*, *Vibe Magazine*, *Huffington Post*, *NPR*, *TEDx* and many digital platforms. She is the co-founder of the Latina feminist collective Chingona Fire and an internationally recognized body positivity activist. Yesika is the author of the Amazon best-sellers *Corazón* and *Tesoro*, published with Not a Cult.